Table of Contents

50 Easy Weekend Scroll Saw Projects

by
John A. Nelson

Fox Chapel Publishing Co., Inc.
1970 Broad Street
East Petersburg, PA 17520

John Nelson and other scrollers throughout the country have teamed up with Fox Chapel Publishing Company, Inc., to create a series of wonderful scroll saw books. This set of books is reasonably priced in order that scrollers can compile a great collection of scroll saw patterns and projects at a minimum cost. (In most cases less than twenty five cents per pattern.)

If you purchase—and like—any one book in this set of books, you should look at other books in the series, as we think you will want the other books as well.

The following people have my gratitude for helping with this book. Without them all this book could never have been published. First of all, to my wife Joyce, who interpreted my horrible writing and poor spelling. She turned my "hen scratching" into an actual manuscript for this book. To Hilary, my ten-year-old granddaughter, for helping Joyce paint many projects. Also, to Bill Ray of Akron, Ohio, and Paul Revere of Florida for helping me make many of the projects. Alan Giagnocavo and staff at Fox Chapel Publishing Company, Inc., without their help this book could not have been published.

I would like to acknowledge and thank those of you who have purchased my book. I sincerely hope you will enjoy our efforts.

John A. Nelson
PO Box 422
Dublin, NH 03444–0422

© 1998 by Fox Chapel Publishing Company, Inc.

Publisher: Alan Giagnocavo
Project Editor: Ayleen Stellhorn

ISBN 1-56523-108-2

To order your copy of this book,
please send check or money order
for $9.95 plus $3.50 shipping to:
Fox Books Orders
1970 Broad Street
East Petersburg, PA 17520

Try your favorite book supplier first!

10 9 8 7 6 5 4 3 2

Basic Instructions

In choosing the wood, be sure to choose an interesting piece of wood, a piece of wood with character and a nice grain pattern to it. (Remember, the _wood_ is the _least_ expensive part of your project --- it is your _time_ cutting and finishing the project that is the actual "cost".)

After carefully choosing wood for your project, cut the wood to overall size.

Sand the top and bottom surfaces with medium sandpaper. Finish up with fine sandpaper.

Make a copy of the pattern at a local copy center. Enlarge or reduce as noted on the drawing.

Because of size limitations, some of the larger patterns had to be cut in half. Simply make copies full-size or enlarged as noted, and line up the two halves and glue them back together. Take care to line up all matching lines. _Note:_ Glue matching letters together, i.e., "X" to "X" and "Y" to "Y", etc.

Attach the pattern to the wood by spraying the pattern with a spray adhesive. Spray the back of the paper _not_ the wood. Let the adhesive set for a minute or two then attach pattern to the wood.

If there are interior cuts, carefully drill small starter holes for the blade to fit through, in each of the interior open areas. Carefully, make all interior cuts. (A #2 or #5 skip-tooth blade is recommended.) Be sure to keep a good sharp corners as you cut. Carefully, make the final outside cut.

Finishing
Sand all over with medium than fine sandpaper. Remove all dust from your project.

If you have to stain your project, try dipping it into a large, flat pan filled with the stain. Remove project and wipe down any excessive stain. (Pour the remaining stain back into the can for later use.) After stain dries, spray with satin or gloss varnish or lacquer, as noted above.

A few projects call for a plastic mirror as a background, simply cut the plastic as you do the wood. Glue in place.

After I have finished a project, I always put a coat of paste wax on the project. This gives your project a nice finish and "feel" to it.

Note: The projects in this book illustrates only one use of each project. Do not limit yourself only to what is suggested, try enlarging or reducing each project, change or modify the designs to create your very own project. You are limited only by your own imagination, experiment - have fun with these patterns.

WINDOW HANGER
PLANT COMPANION

NOTE:
MANY WINDOW HANGER PATTERNS CAN BE
ENLARGED TO ABOUT 6" TO 8" IN DIAMETER
AND BE USED AS A TRIVET--USE 5/8" TO
3/4" THICK HARDWOOD FOR TRIVETS

1/8 TO 1/4 TK.

WINDOW HANGER

STACK-CUT TO SAVE TIME

1/8 TO 1/4 TK.

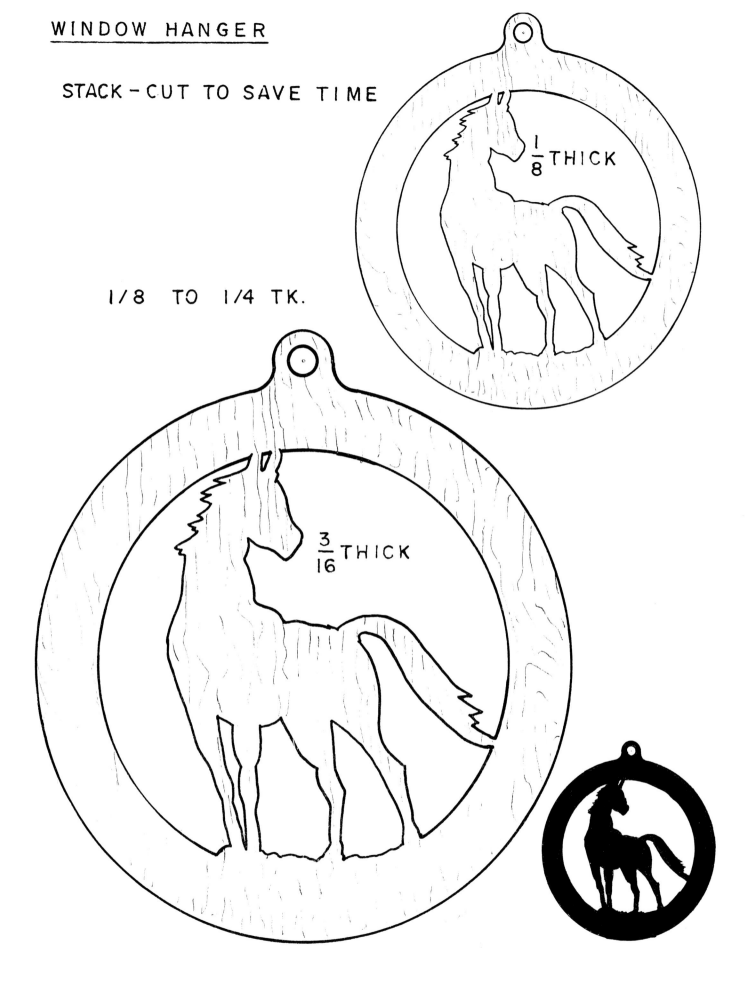

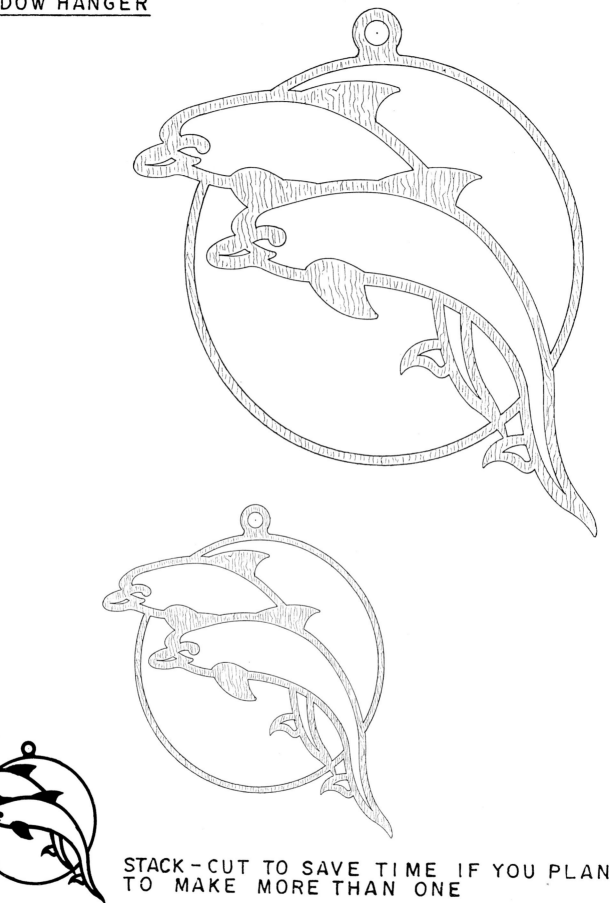

STACK-CUT TO SAVE TIME IF YOU PLAN
TO MAKE MORE THAN ONE

WINDOW HANGER

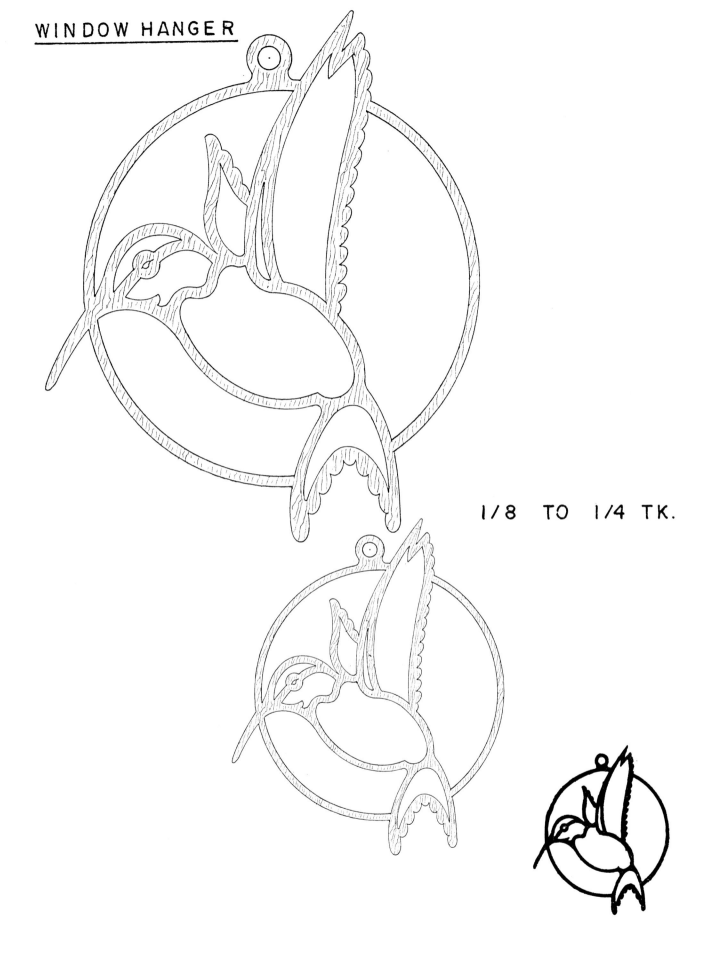

1/8 TO 1/4 TK.

1/8 TO 1/4 TK.

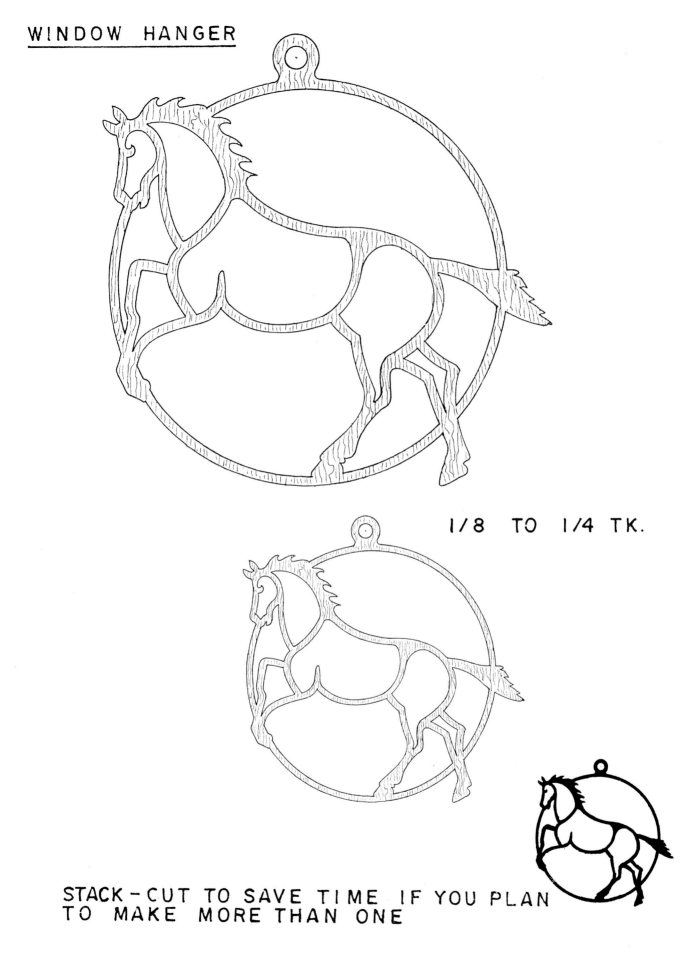

1/8 TO 1/4 TK.

STACK-CUT TO SAVE TIME IF YOU PLAN
TO MAKE MORE THAN ONE

KEY HANGER & SHELF

1/4 TK.

ADD SMALL HOOKS(5)

SHELF
1/4 TK.

50 EASY WEEKEND Scroll Saw Projects

PLANT COMPANION

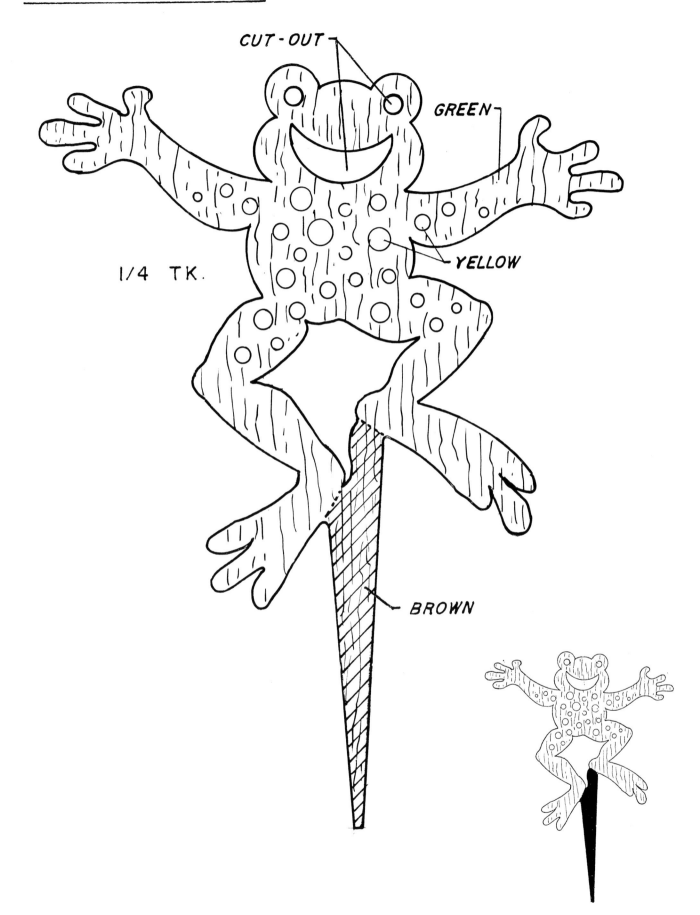

CUT-OUT

GREEN

YELLOW

1/4 TK.

BROWN

PLANT COMPANION

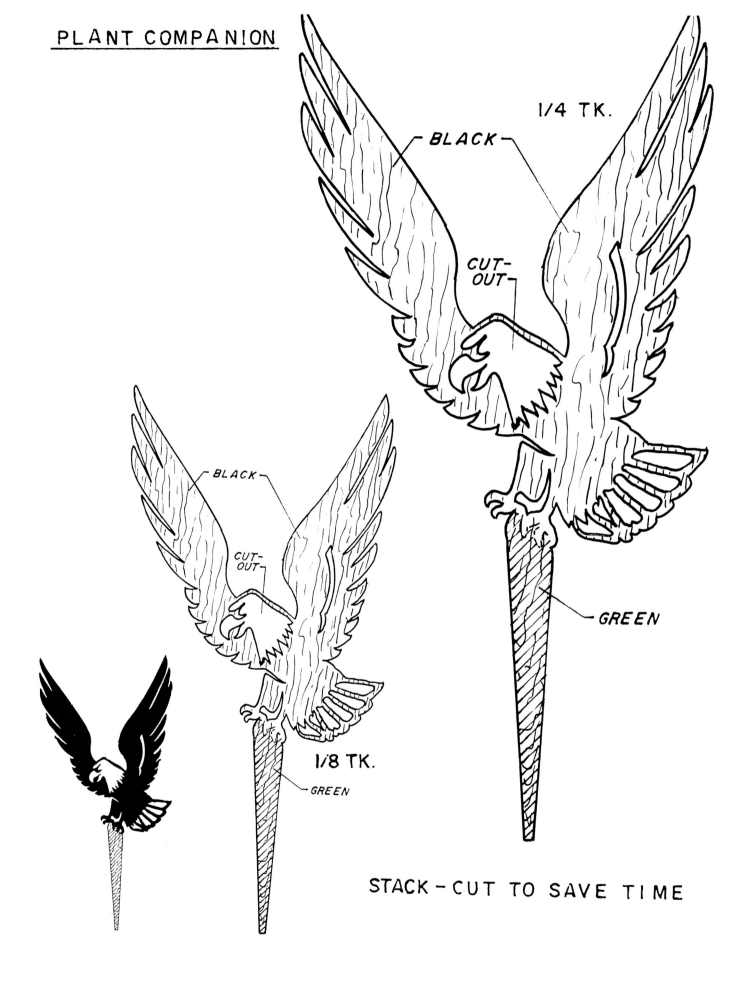

1/4 TK.

BLACK

CUT-OUT

BLACK

CUT-OUT

GREEN

1/8 TK.

GREEN

STACK—CUT TO SAVE TIME

BOOK MARKER

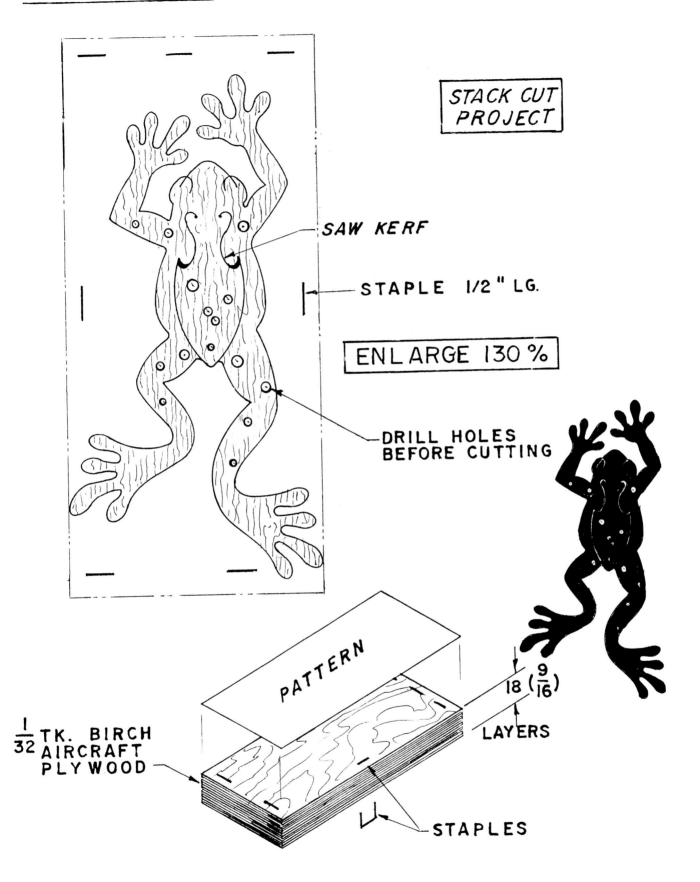

STACK CUT PROJECT

SAW KERF

STAPLE 1/2" LG.

ENLARGE 130%

DRILL HOLES BEFORE CUTTING

PATTERN

$18 \left(\frac{9}{16}\right)$ LAYERS

$\frac{1}{32}$ TK. BIRCH AIRCRAFT PLYWOOD

STAPLES

HOT PLATE STAND

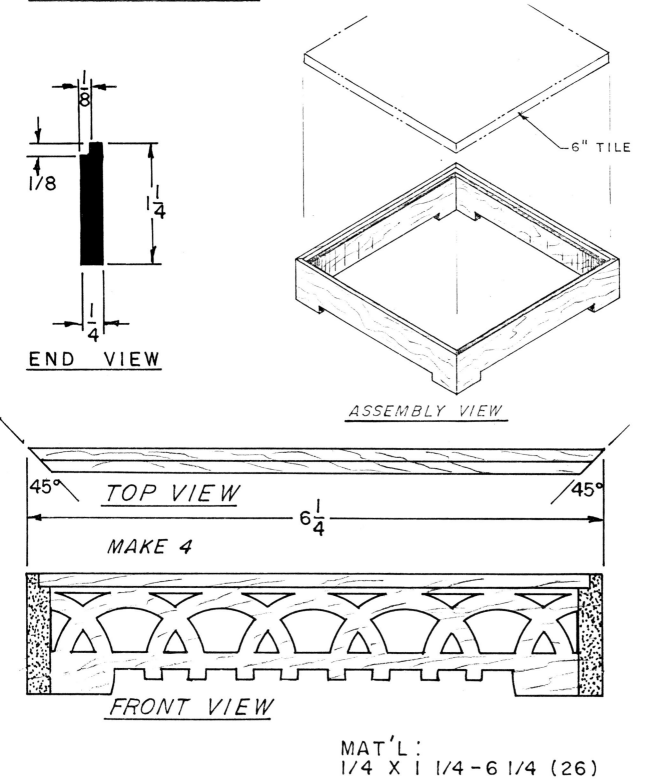

$\frac{1}{8}$

1/8

$1\frac{1}{4}$

$\frac{1}{4}$

END VIEW

6" TILE

ASSEMBLY VIEW

45°   TOP VIEW   45°

$6\frac{1}{4}$

MAKE 4

FRONT VIEW

MAT'L:
1/4 X 1 1/4 - 6 1/4 (26)

TRIVETS

(CHINESE CHARACTERS)

1/2 TO 3/4 TK.

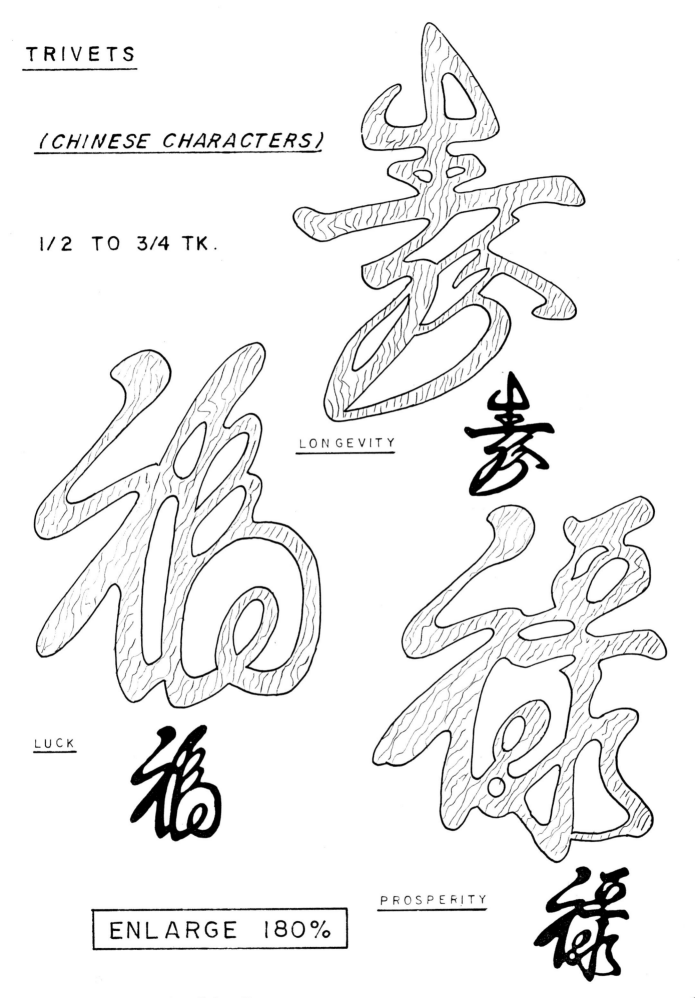

LONGEVITY

LUCK

PROSPERITY

ENLARGE 180%

BUSNESS CARD HOLDER

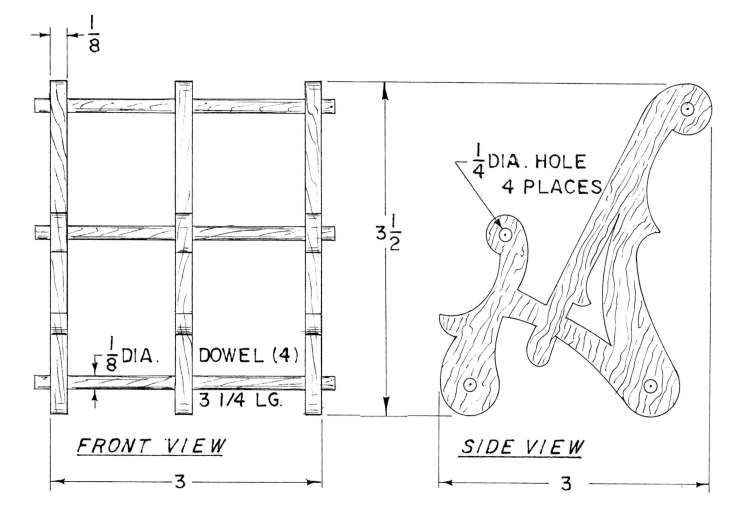

$\frac{1}{8}$

$3\frac{1}{2}$

$\frac{1}{8}$ DIA.   DOWEL (4)

3 1/4 LG.

FRONT VIEW

3

$\frac{1}{4}$ DIA. HOLE
4 PLACES

SIDE VIEW

3

PUZZLE

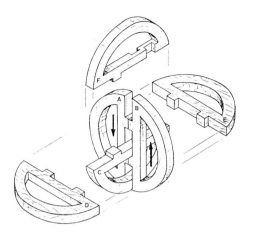

ASSEMBLY

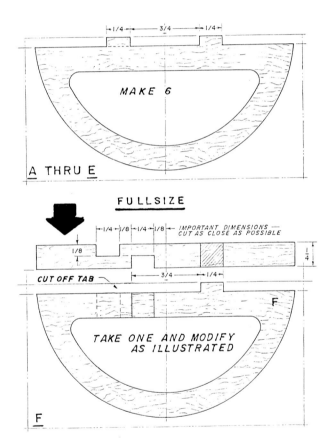

|←1/4→| ← 3/4 → |←1/4→|

MAKE 6

A THRU E

FULLSIZE

|1/4|1/8|1/4|1/8| IMPORTANT DIMENSIONS —
CUT AS CLOSE AS POSSIBLE

1/8

1/4

3/4   1/4

CUT OFF TAB

F

TAKE ONE AND MODIFY
AS ILLUSTRATED

F

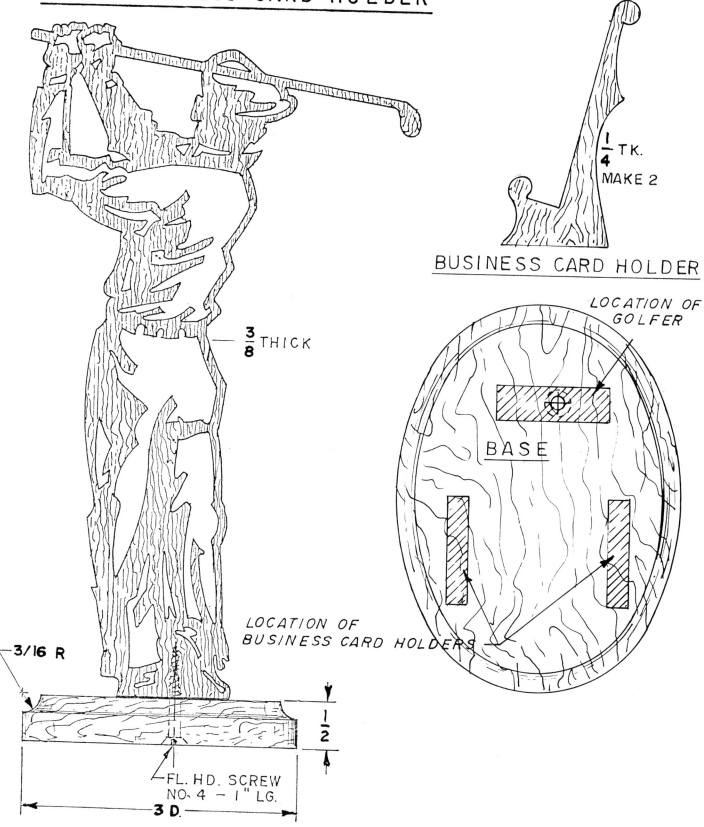

$\frac{1}{4}$ TK.
MAKE 2

BUSINESS CARD HOLDER

$\frac{3}{8}$ THICK

LOCATION OF
GOLFER

BASE

LOCATION OF
BUSINESS CARD HOLDERS

3/16 R

$\frac{1}{2}$

FL. HD. SCREW
NO. 4 — 1" LG.

3 D.

GOLFER FOR THE DESK

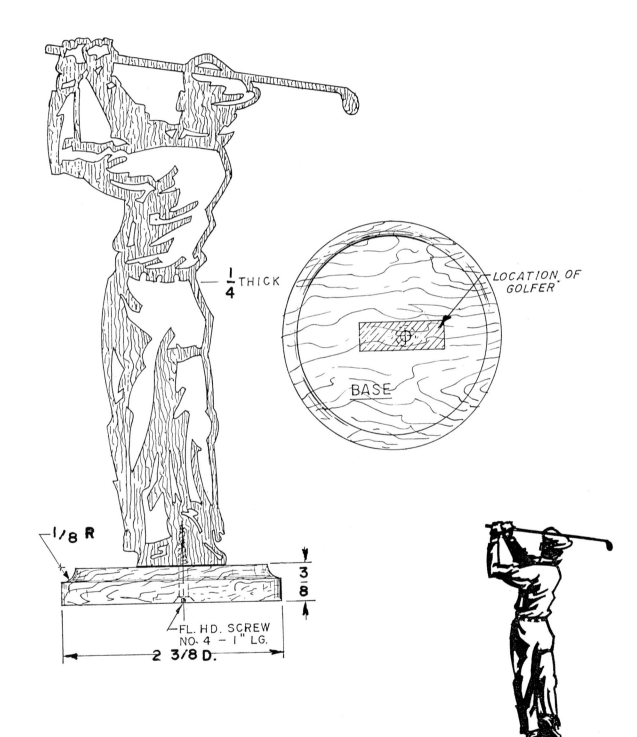

$\frac{1}{4}$ THICK

LOCATION OF GOLFER

BASE

1/8 R

$\frac{3}{8}$

FL. HD. SCREW
NO. 4 - 1" LG.

2 3/8 D.

PAPERWEIGHT DESK CLOCK

FIT-UP 1 7/16
1 3/8 DIA. HOLE
5/16 DP.

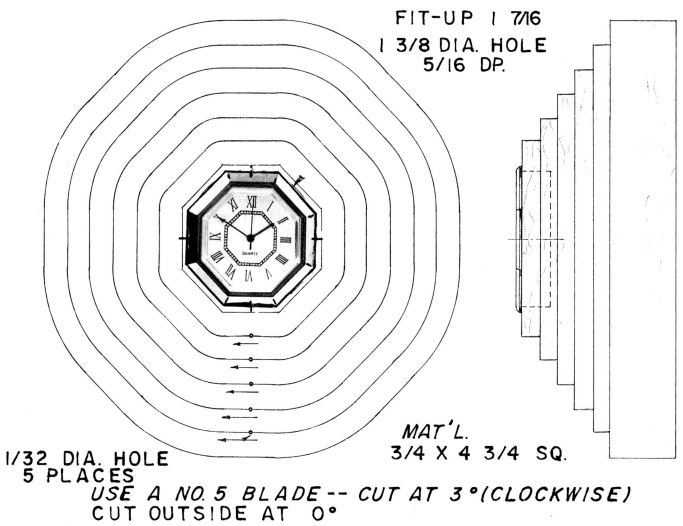

1/32 DIA. HOLE
5 PLACES

MAT'L.
3/4 X 4 3/4 SQ.

USE A NO. 5 BLADE -- CUT AT 3°(CLOCKWISE)
CUT OUTSIDE AT 0°

KEY HANGER

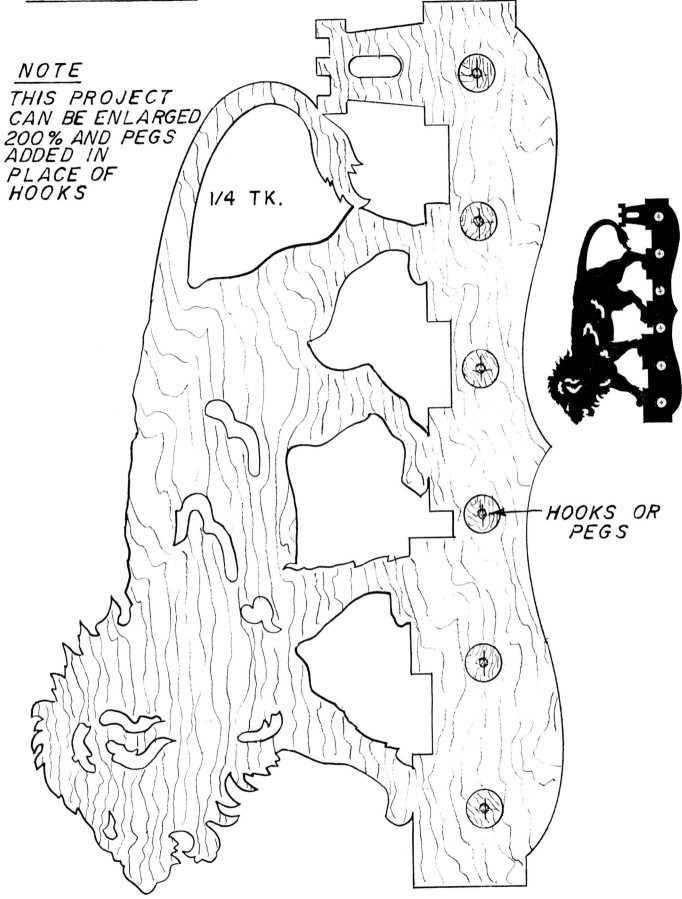

NOTE
THIS PROJECT
CAN BE ENLARGED
200% AND PEGS
ADDED IN
PLACE OF
HOOKS

1/4 TK.

HOOKS OR
PEGS

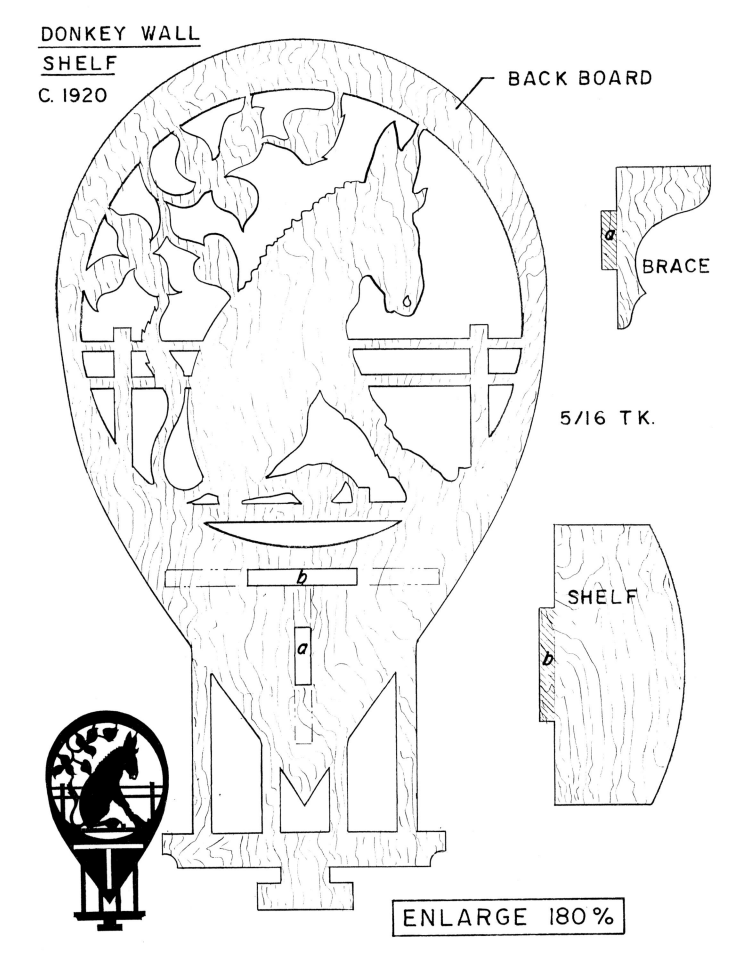

DONKEY WALL
SHELF
C. 1920

BACK BOARD

BRACE

5/16 TK.

a

SHELF

b

b

a

ENLARGE 180%

DUCKY WALL
SHELF
C. 1920

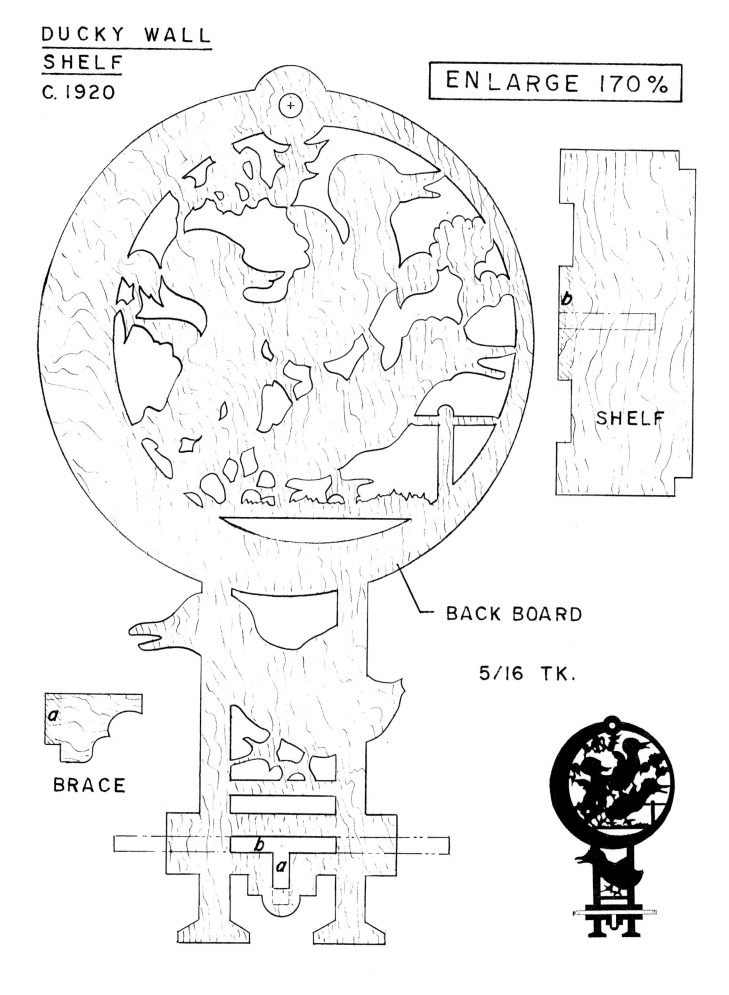

ENLARGE 170%

SHELF

BACK BOARD

5/16 TK.

BRACE

PUPPY LOVE WALL SHELF

BACK BOARD

b

a

*FRONT
VIEW*

50 EASY WEEKEND Scroll Saw Projects

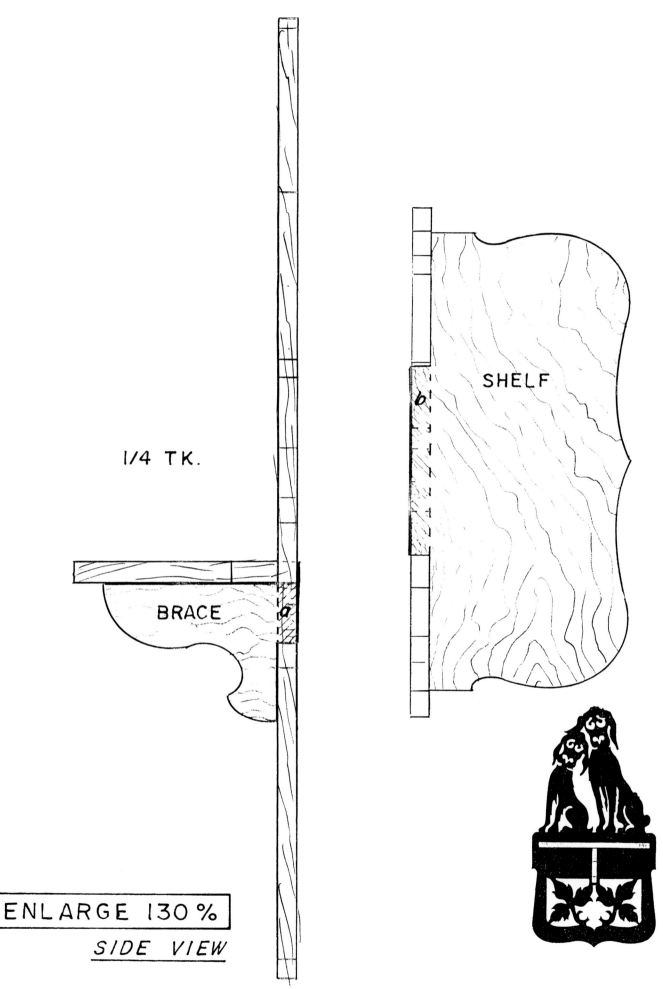

1/4 TK.

BRACE

a

SHELF

b

ENLARGE 130%

SIDE VIEW

TRAIN WALL
PLAQUE

OPTIONAL—
ADD A CLOTH
& MIRROR
BACKING

3/8 TK.

ENLARGE 150%

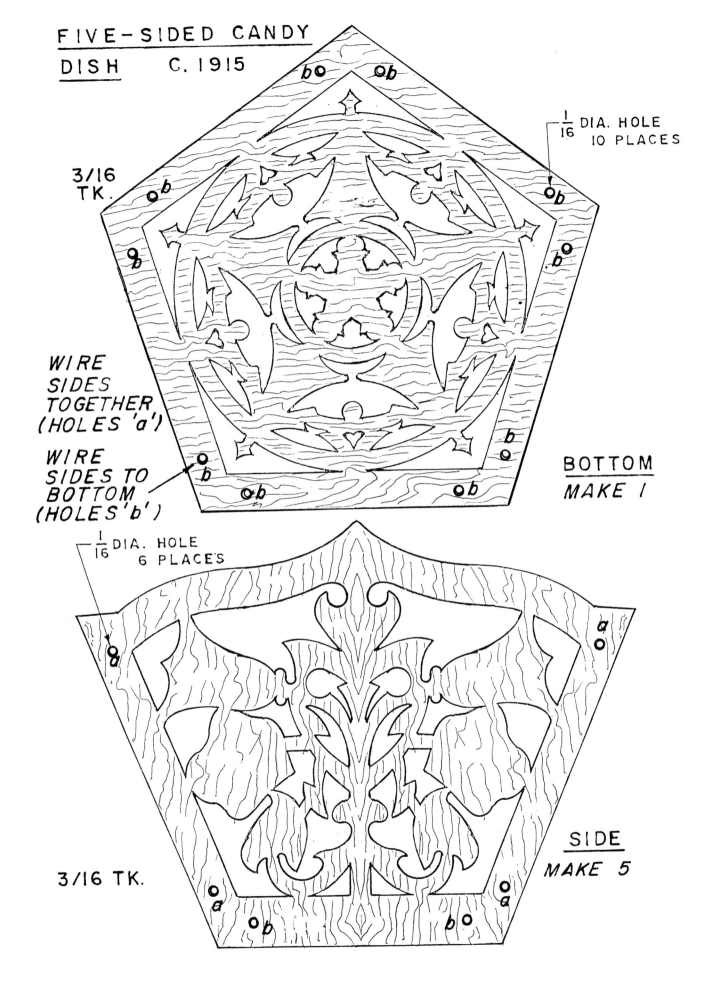

FIVE-SIDED CANDY
DISH   C. 1915

b○   ○b

$\frac{1}{16}$ DIA. HOLE
10 PLACES

3/16
TK.

○b

b○

○b

b○

WIRE
SIDES
TOGETHER
(HOLES 'a')

WIRE
SIDES TO
BOTTOM
(HOLES 'b')

○b

b○

○b

BOTTOM
MAKE 1

○b   b○

$\frac{1}{16}$ DIA. HOLE
6 PLACES

a○

a○

a○

3/16 TK.

a○

○a

○b   b○

SIDE
MAKE 5

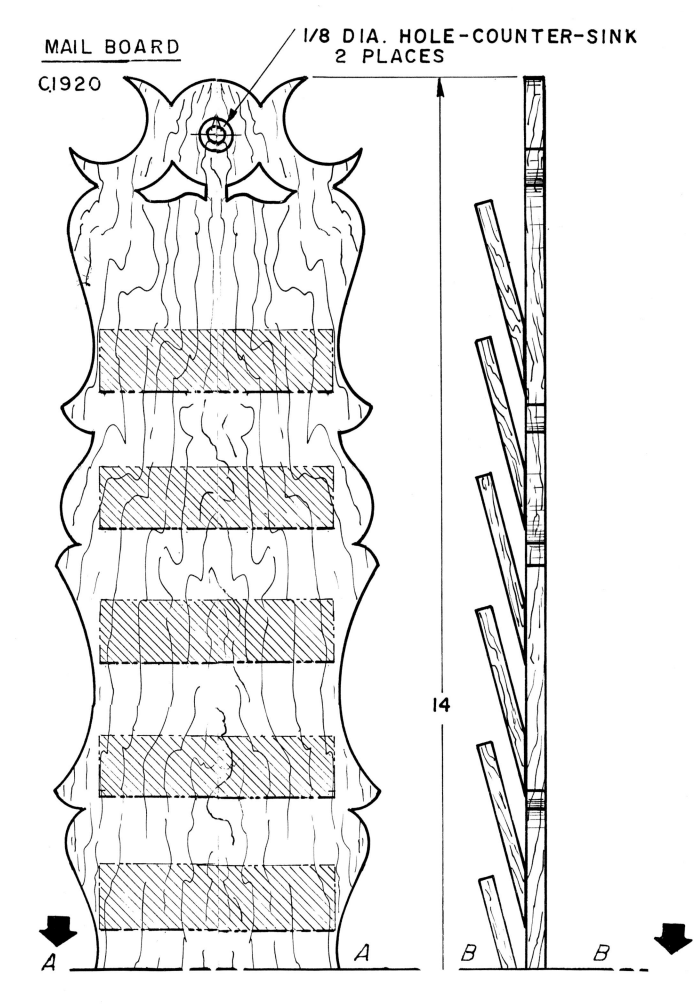

MAIL BOARD

C.1920

1/8 DIA. HOLE-COUNTER-SINK
2 PLACES

14

A   A   B   B

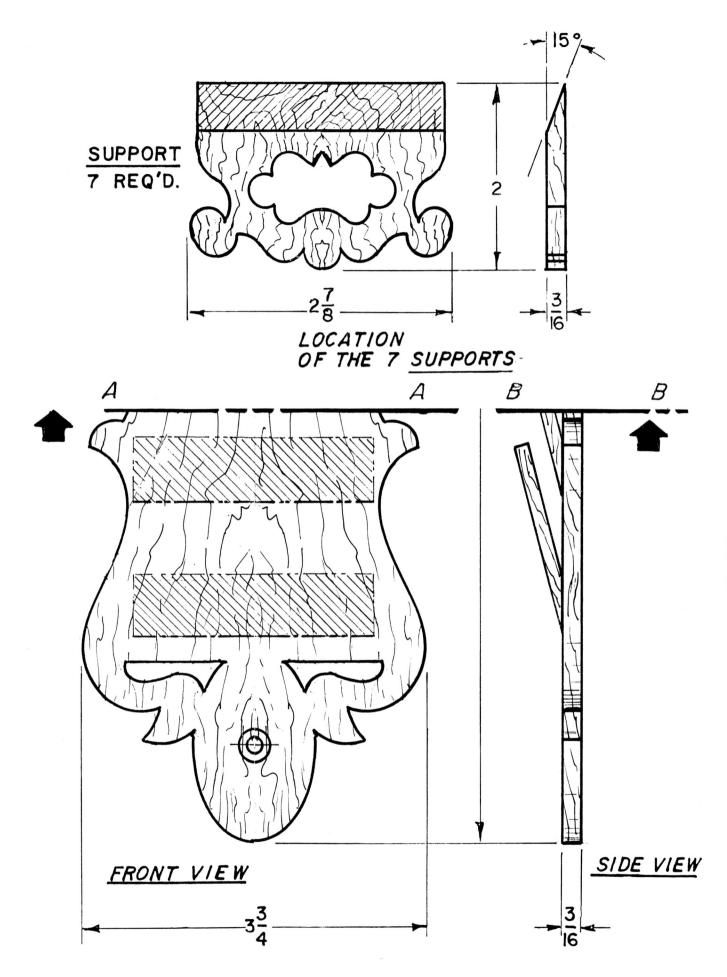

SUPPORT
7 REQ'D.

15°

2

3/16

LOCATION
OF THE 7 SUPPORTS

A   A   B   B

2 7/8

FRONT VIEW

SIDE VIEW

3 3/4

3/16

WASTEPAPER BASKET

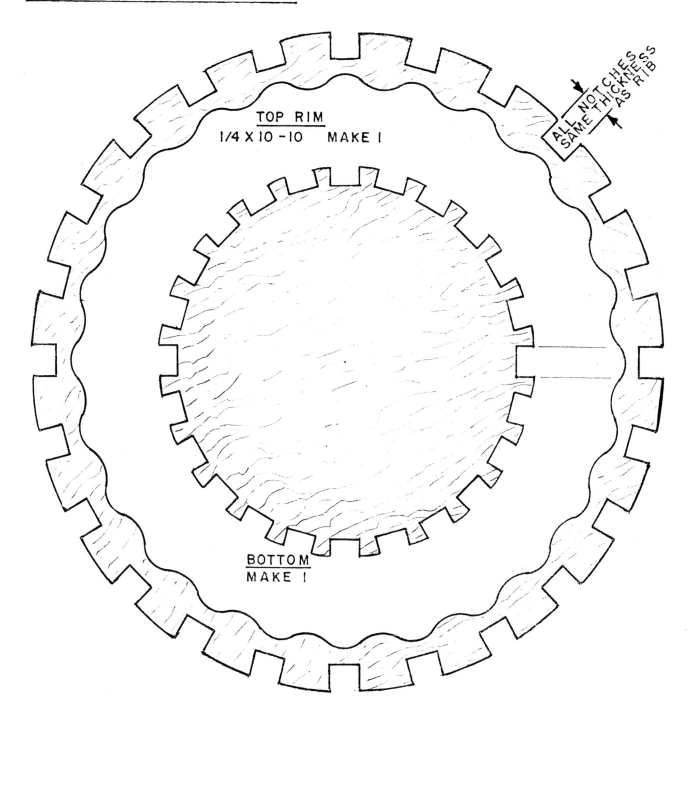

TOP RIM
1/4 X 10 -10   MAKE I

ALL NOTCHES
SAME THICKNESS
AS RIB

BOTTOM
MAKE I

ENLARGE 145 %

CENTER

TOP RIM —

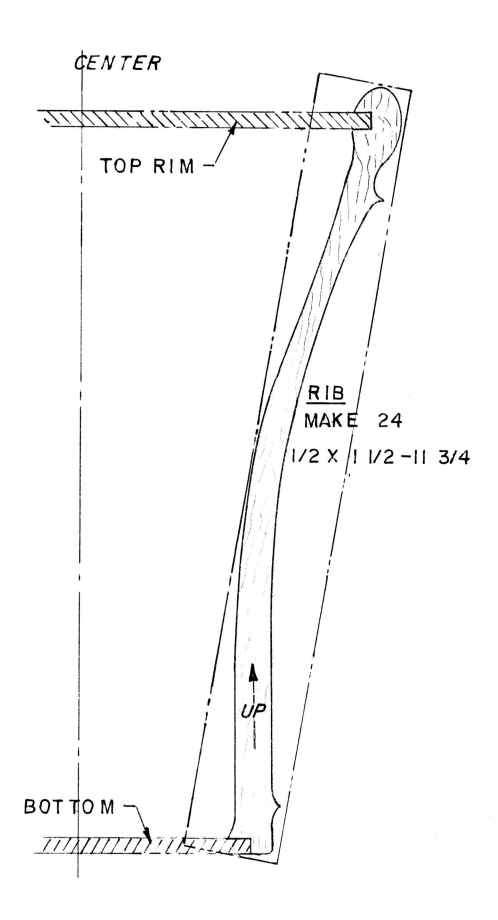

RIB
MAKE 24
1/2 X 1 1/2 – 11 3/4

UP

BOTTOM —

PLANT STAND

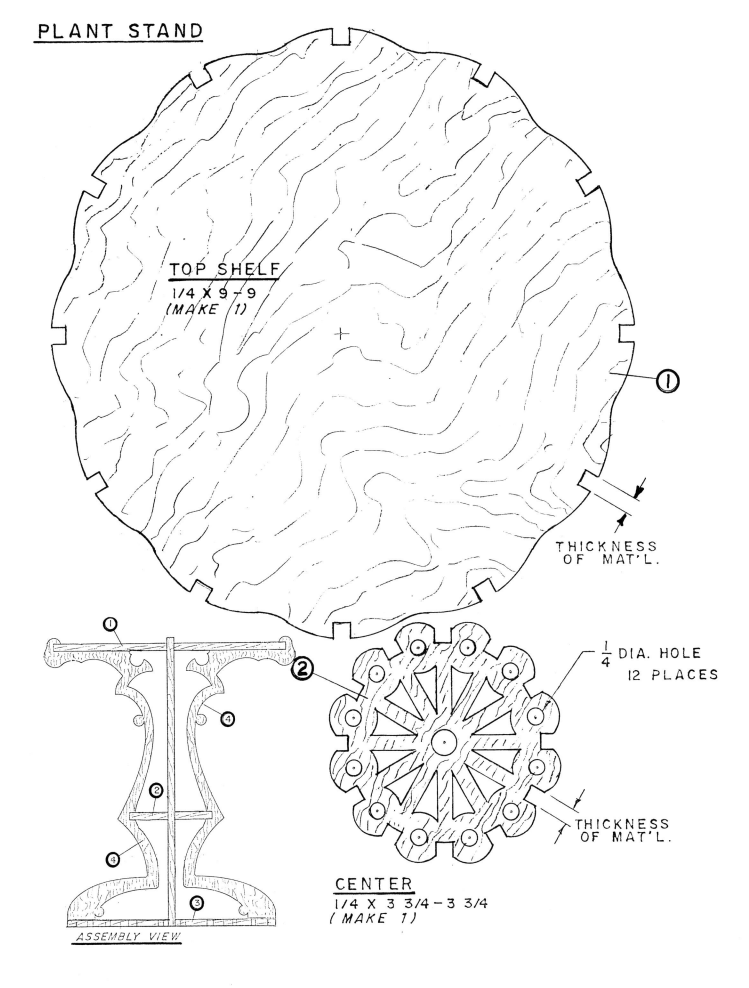

TOP SHELF
1/4 X 9 – 9
(MAKE 1)

①

THICKNESS
OF MAT'L.

②

④

②

④

③

ASSEMBLY VIEW

1/4 DIA. HOLE
12 PLACES

THICKNESS
OF MAT'L.

CENTER
1/4 X 3 3/4 – 3 3/4
(MAKE 1)

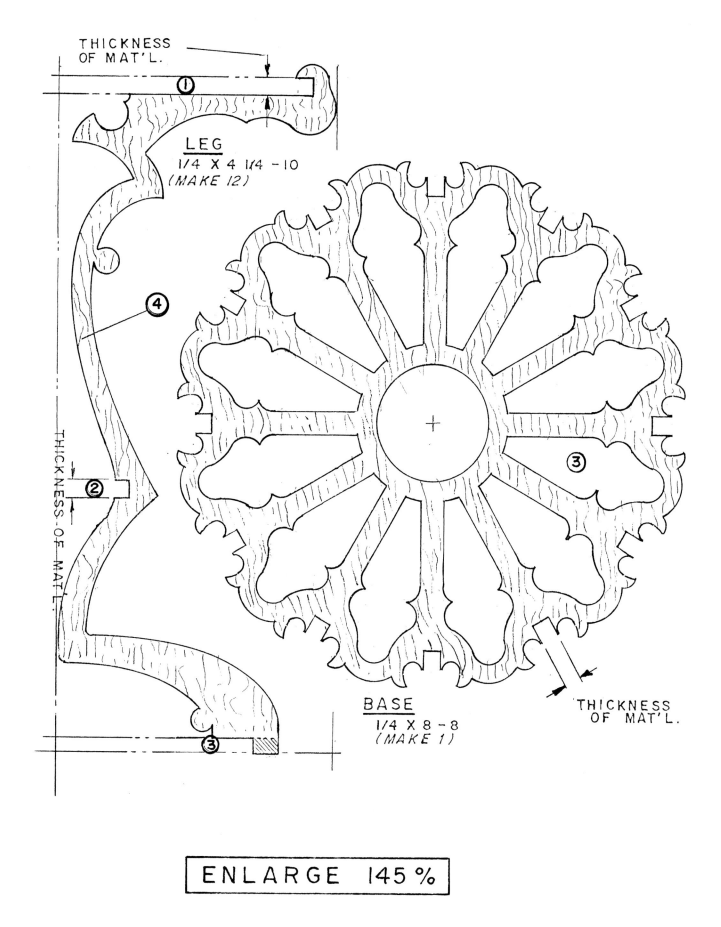

THICKNESS OF MAT'L.

LEG
1/4 X 4 1/4 -10
(MAKE 12)

④

THICKNESS OF MAT'L.

②

①

③

③

BASE
1/4 X 8 - 8
(MAKE 1)

THICKNESS
OF MAT'L.

ENLARGE 145%

FLOWER POT STAND

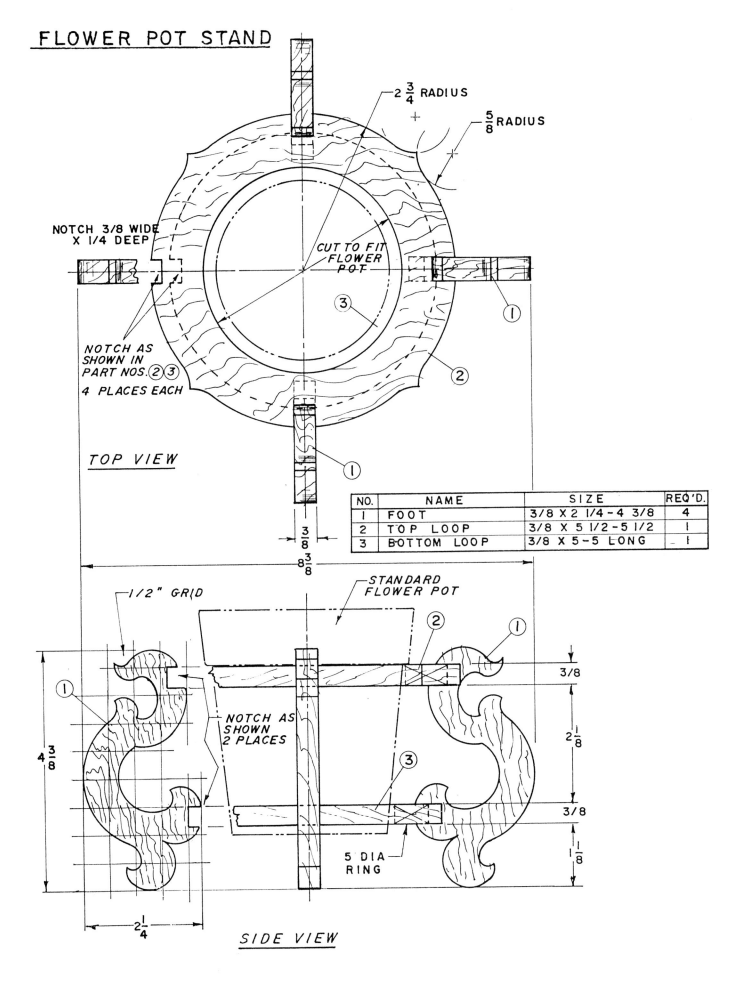

TOP VIEW

2 ¾ RADIUS

⅝ RADIUS

CUT TO FIT FLOWER POT

NOTCH 3/8 WIDE X 1/4 DEEP

NOTCH AS SHOWN IN PART NOS. ②③ 4 PLACES EACH

NO.	NAME	SIZE	REQ'D.
1	FOOT	3/8 X 2 1/4 - 4 3/8	4
2	TOP LOOP	3/8 X 5 1/2 - 5 1/2	1
3	BOTTOM LOOP	3/8 X 5 - 5 LONG	1

3/8

8 ⅜

1/2" GRID

STANDARD FLOWER POT

NOTCH AS SHOWN 2 PLACES

3/8

2 ⅛

3/8

1 ⅛

5 DIA RING

4 ⅜

2 ¼

SIDE VIEW

PLANT STAND ON WHEELS

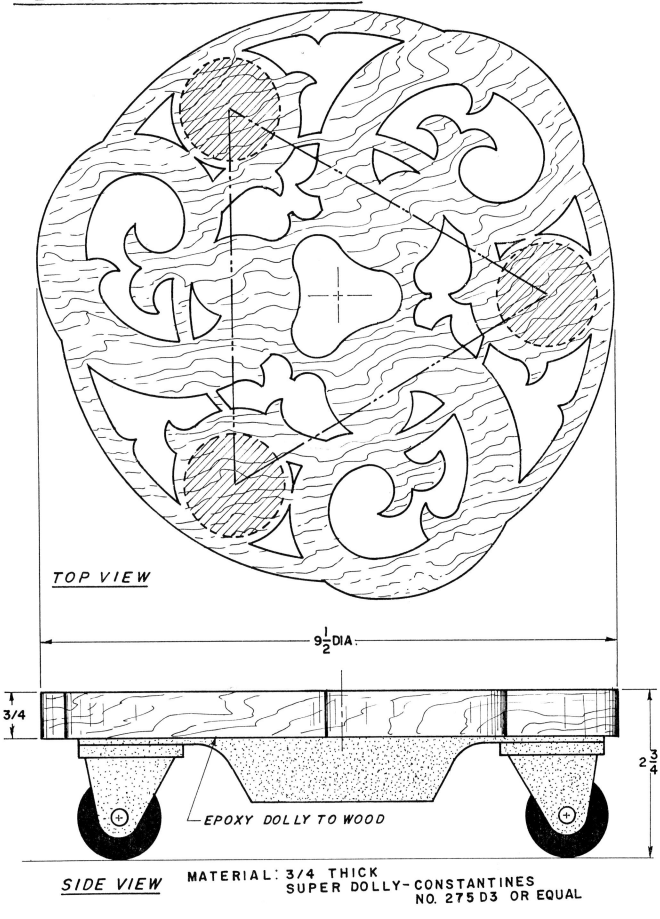

TOP VIEW

9½ DIA

3/4

2¾

EPOXY DOLLY TO WOOD

SIDE VIEW   MATERIAL: 3/4 THICK
SUPER DOLLY-CONSTANTINES
NO. 275 D3 OR EQUAL

DRY FLOWER POT

D 1/8 TK.
MAKE 2

DARK STAIN

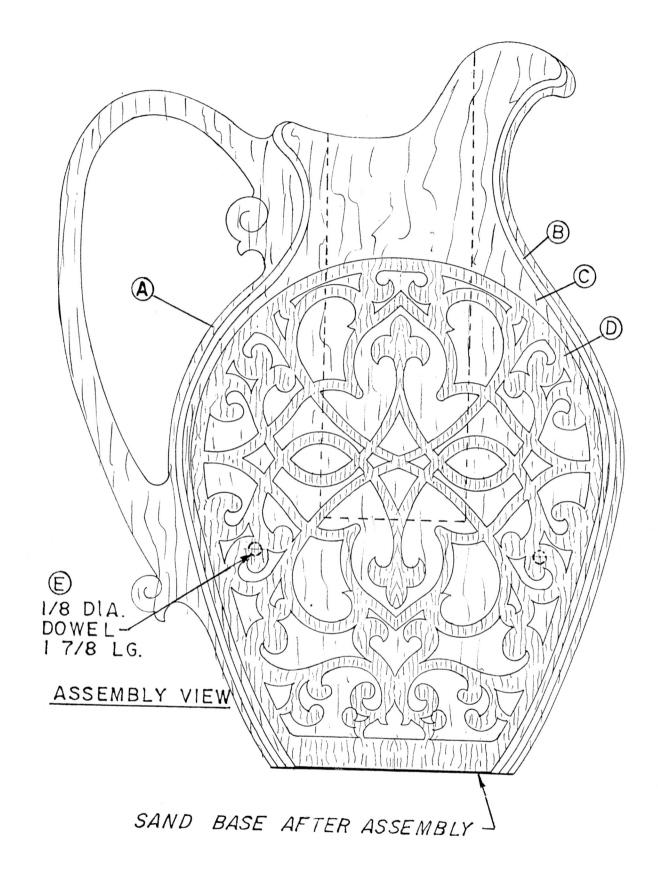

Ⓐ

Ⓑ

Ⓒ

Ⓓ

Ⓔ
1/8 DIA.
DOWEL
1 7/8 LG.

ASSEMBLY VIEW

SAND BASE AFTER ASSEMBLY

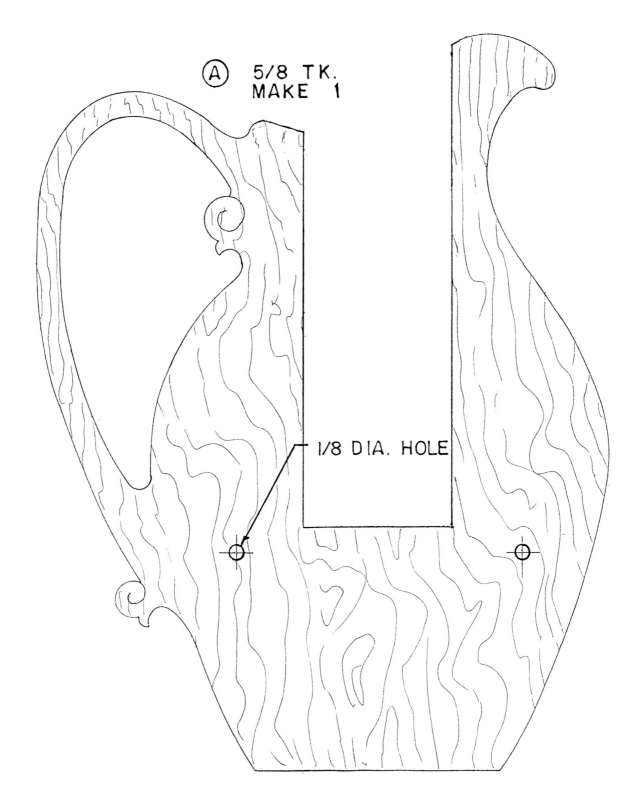

(A) 5/8 TK.
MAKE 1

1/8 DIA. HOLE

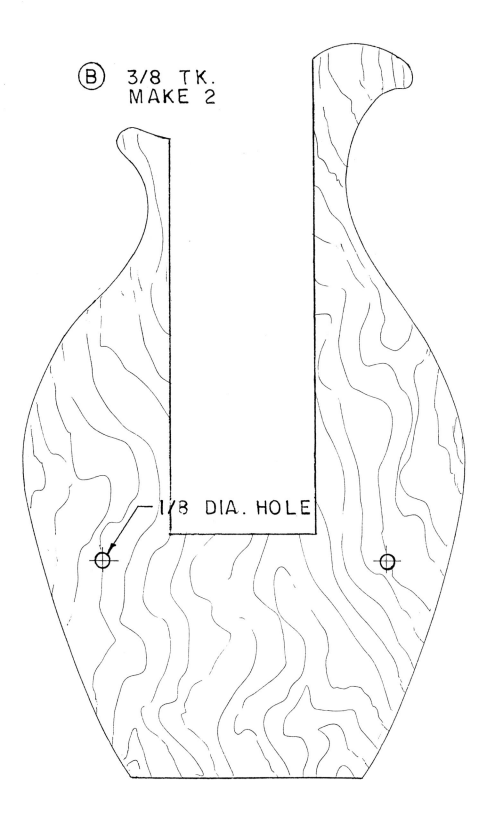

Ⓑ 3/8 TK.
MAKE 2

—1/8 DIA. HOLE

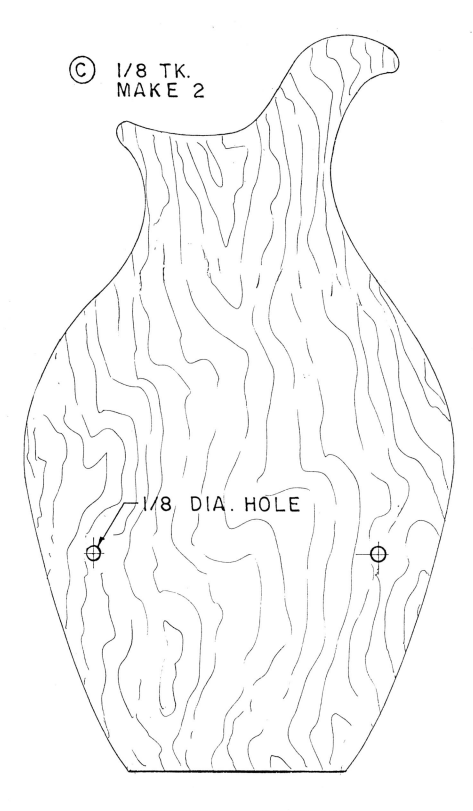

© 1/8 TK.
MAKE 2

1/8 DIA. HOLE

CORNER SHELF
C. 1930

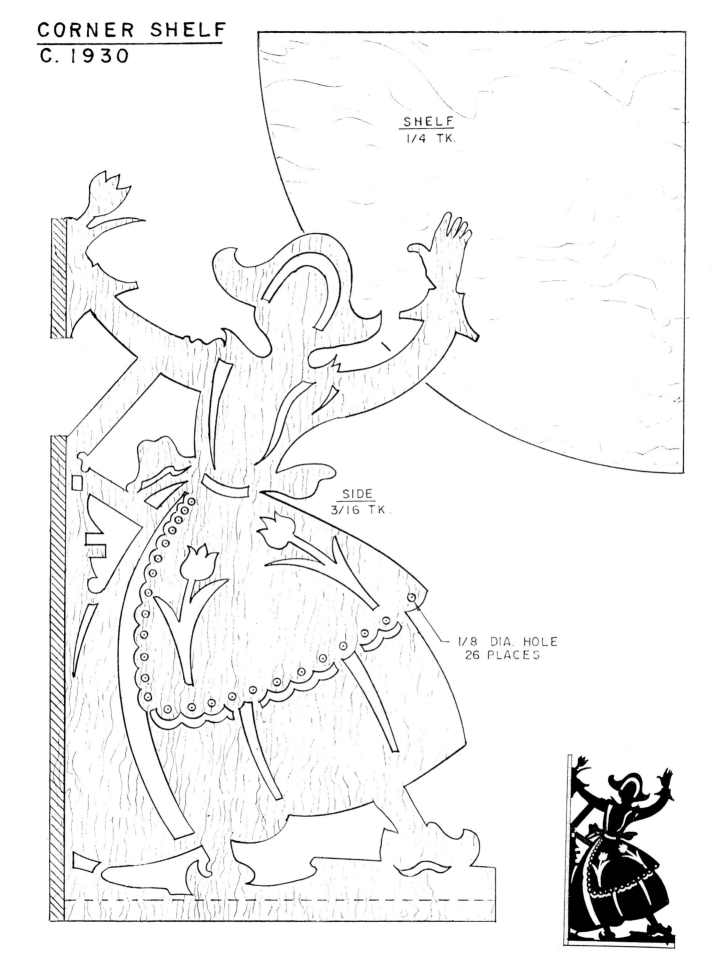

SHELF
1/4 TK.

SIDE
3/16 TK.

1/8 DIA. HOLE
26 PLACES

MAIL WALL HOLDER
C. 1910 (F. J. HAMMER)

ENLARGE 150 %

3/16 TK.

BACKBOARD

FRONT

3/16 TK.

L. SIDE

R. SIDE

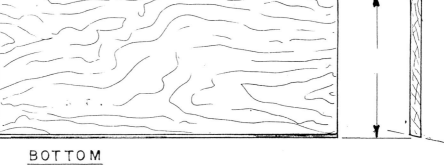

BOTTOM

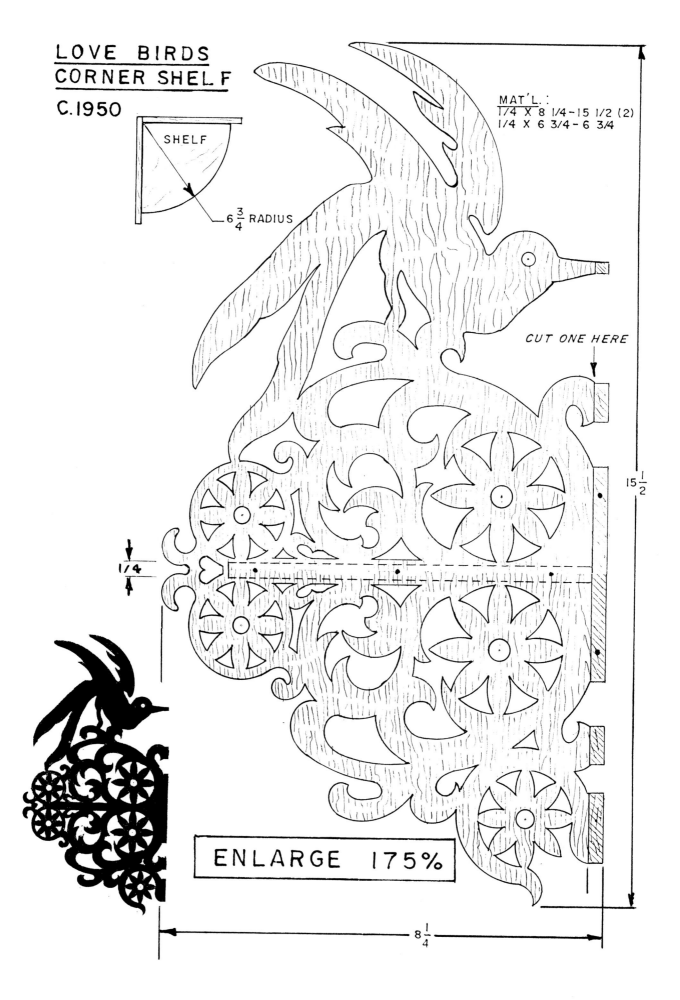

LOVE BIRDS
CORNER SHELF

C.1950

SHELF

6 3/4 RADIUS

MAT'L.:
1/4 X 8 1/4 - 15 1/2 (2)
1/4 X 6 3/4 - 6 3/4

CUT ONE HERE

15 1/2

1/4

ENLARGE 175%

8 1/4

CORNER SHELF

BUTT JOINT

TOP SHELF

BOTTOM SHELF

TOP VIEW

3/4 LG. BRAD

TOP SHELF
1/4 X 5 1/2 - 5 1/2

ENLARGE 165%

15 1/2

BOTTOM VIEW
1/4 X 6 - 6

SIDE VIEW

CUT 1/4" OFF ONE BACKBOARD

1/4

7 1/2

WALL SHELF

1/4 DIA. HOLE

HALF ROUN
SHELF

1/64 DIA. HOL
6 PLACES

SHAPE OF BRACE

BRACE

ENLARGE 145%

50 EASY WEEKEND Scroll Saw Projects

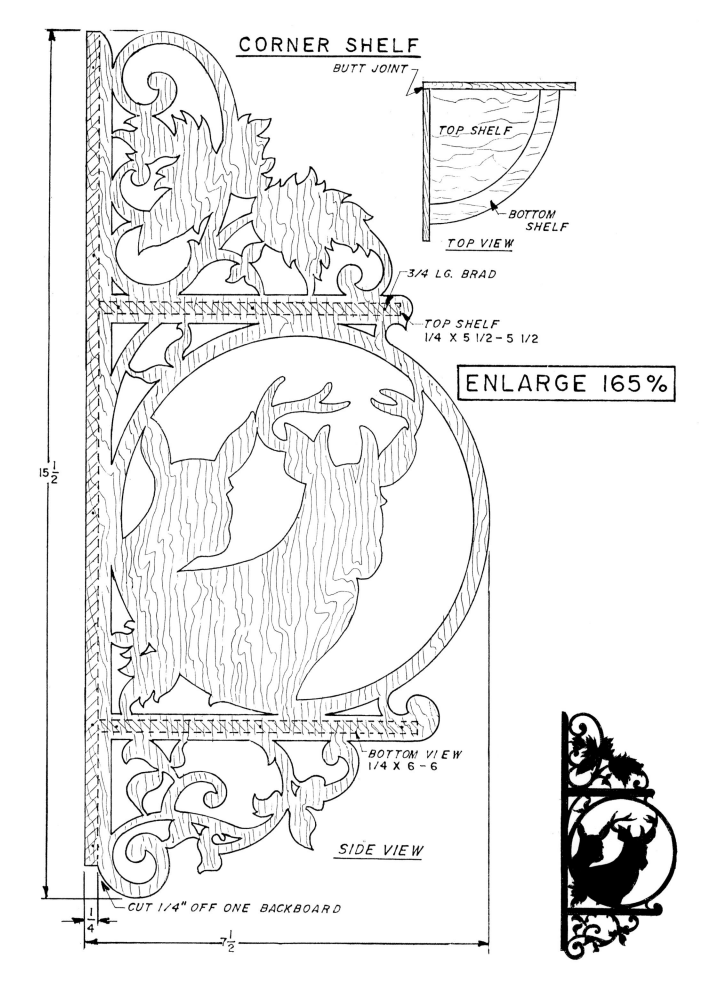

CORNER SHELF

BUTT JOINT

TOP SHELF

BOTTOM SHELF

TOP VIEW

3/4 LG. BRAD

TOP SHELF
1/4 X 5 1/2 - 5 1/2

ENLARGE 165%

15 1/2

BOTTOM VIEW
1/4 X 6 - 6

SIDE VIEW

CUT 1/4" OFF ONE BACKBOARD

1/4

7 1/2

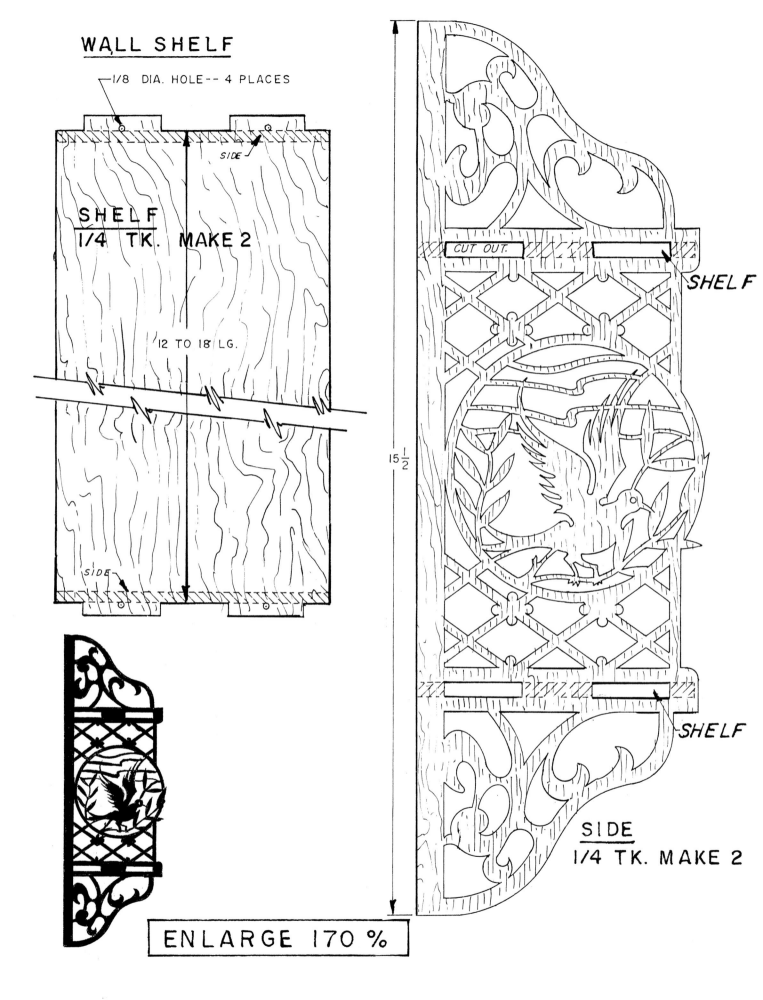

WALL SHELF

−1/8 DIA. HOLE −− 4 PLACES

SHELF
1/4 TK. MAKE 2

12 TO 18 LG.

SIDE

SIDE

15 1/2

CUT OUT.

SHELF

SHELF

SIDE
1/4 TK. MAKE 2

ENLARGE 170 %

WALL SHELF   C. 1920

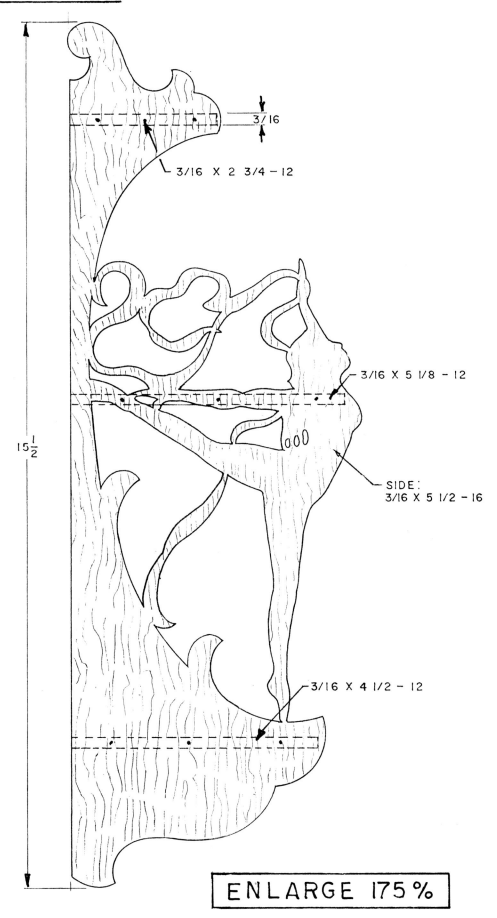

3/16

3/16 X 2 3/4 — 12

3/16 X 5 1/8 — 12

SIDE:
3/16 X 5 1/2 — 16

15 1/2

3/16 X 4 1/2 — 12

ENLARGE 175%

JEWELRY BOX   C.1920

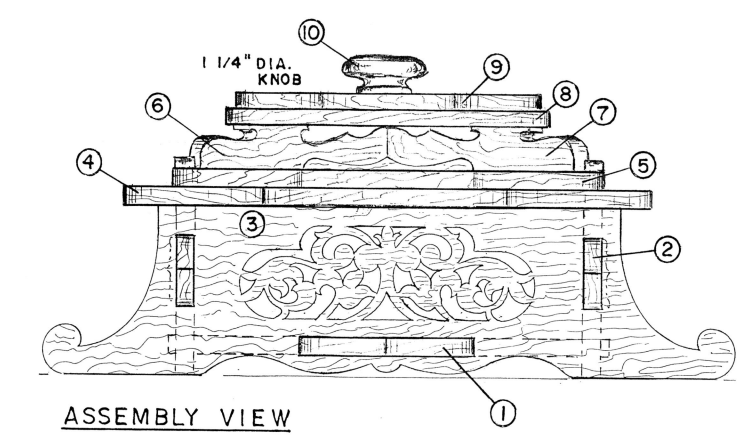

1 1/4" DIA. KNOB

ASSEMBLY VIEW

① BASE
1/4 TK. / MAKE 1

② END
1/4 TK. MAKE 2

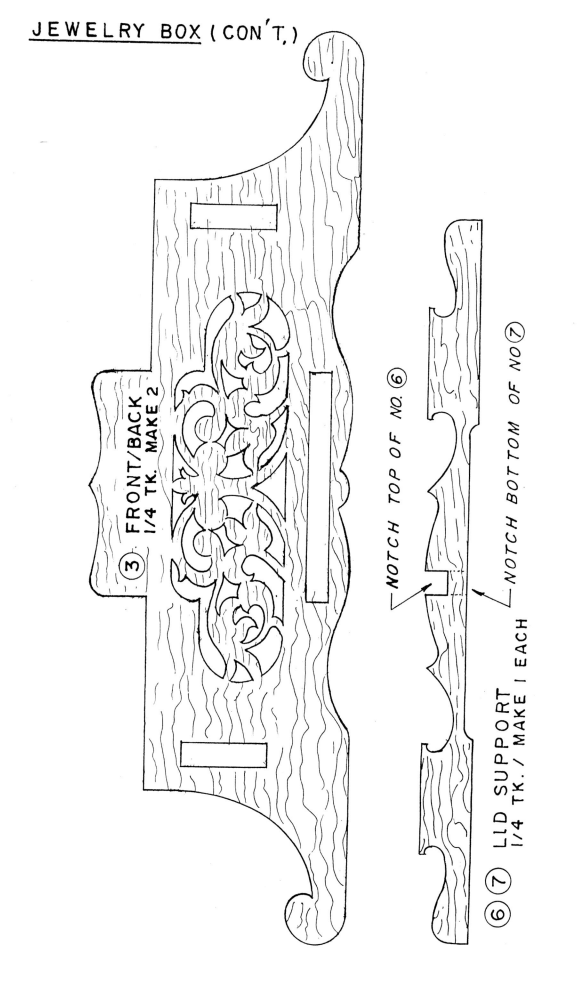

③ FRONT/BACK
1/4 TK. MAKE 2

NOTCH TOP OF NO. ⑥

NOTCH BOTTOM OF NO ⑦

⑥ ⑦ LID SUPPORT
1/4 TK. / MAKE 1 EACH

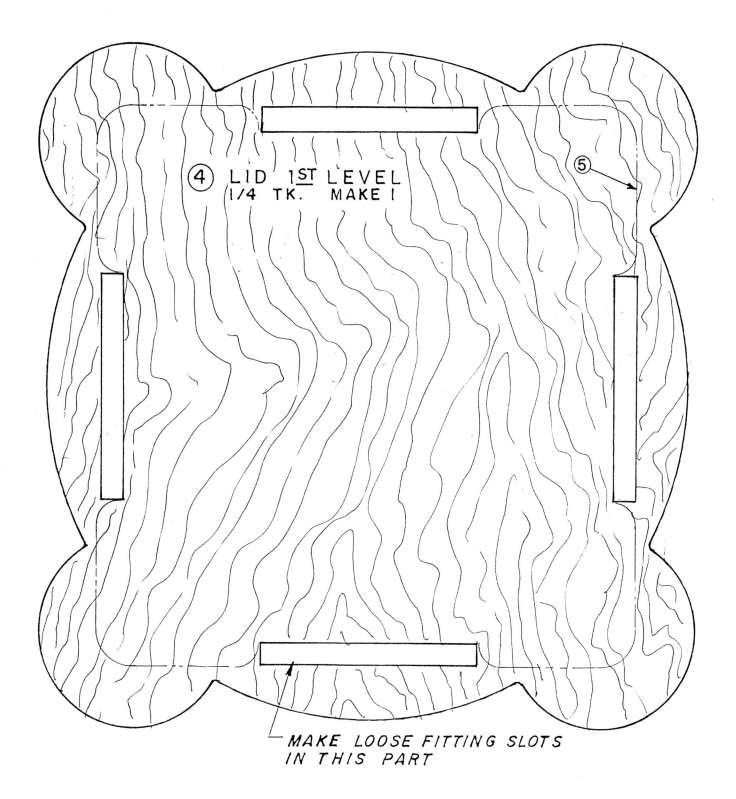

④ LID 1ST LEVEL
1/4 TK. MAKE I

⑤

— MAKE LOOSE FITTING SLOTS
IN THIS PART

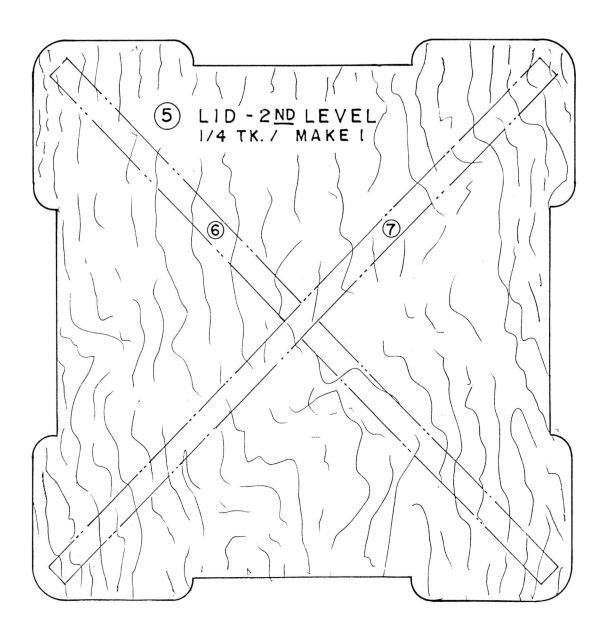

⑤ LID - 2ND LEVEL
1/4 TK. / MAKE 1

⑥   ⑦

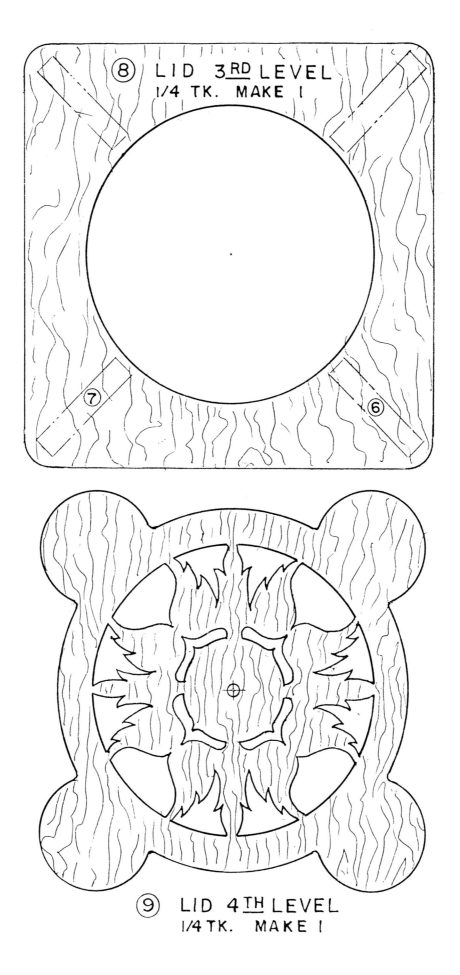

⑧ LID 3RD LEVEL
1/4 TK. MAKE I

⑦

⑥

⑨ LID 4TH LEVEL
1/4 TK. MAKE I

VICTORIAN PICTURE FRAME   C.1890

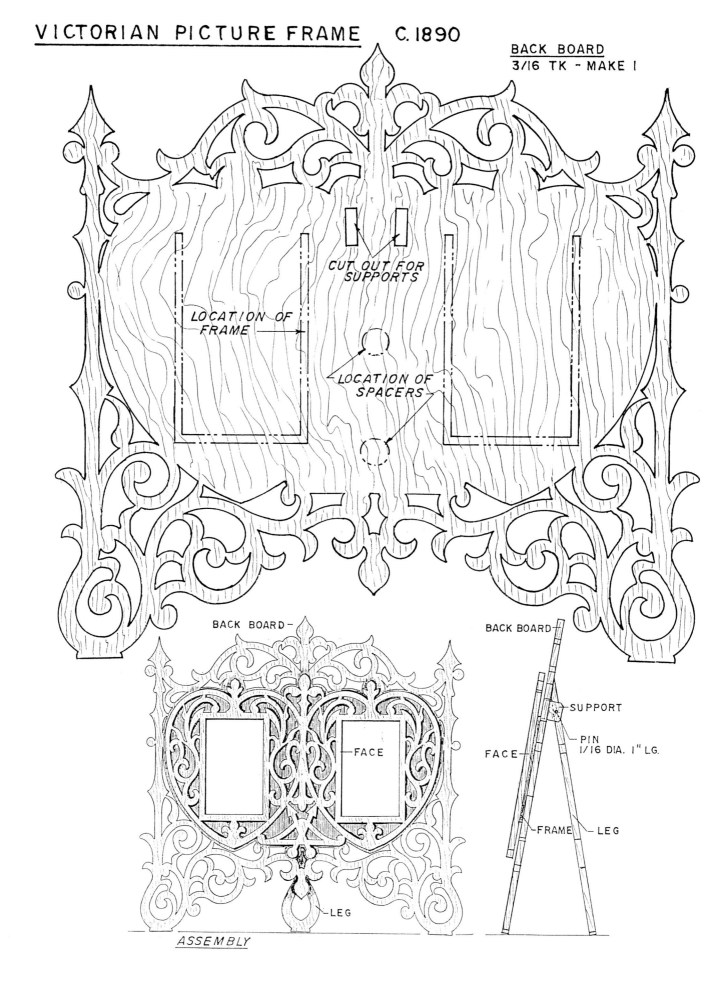

CUT OUT FOR
SUPPORTS

LOCATION OF
FRAME

LOCATION OF
SPACERS

BACK BOARD ~

FACE

LEG

ASSEMBLY

BACK BOARD

SUPPORT

PIN
1/16 DIA. 1" LG.

FACE

FRAME ~~ LEG

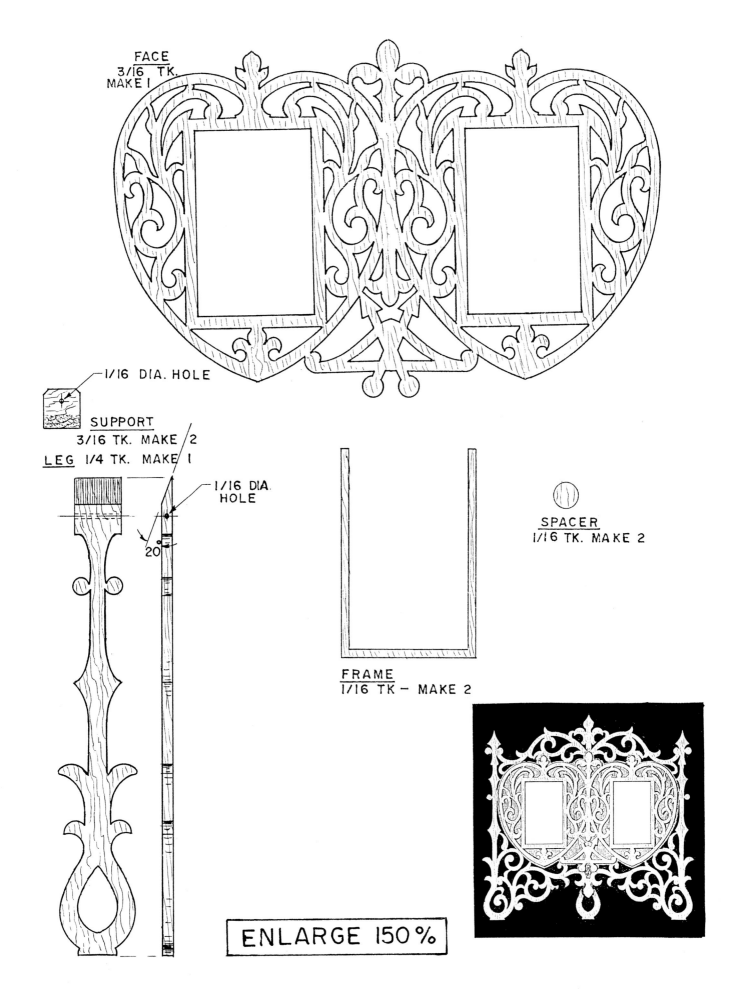

FACE
3/16 TK.
MAKE 1

1/16 DIA. HOLE

SUPPORT
3/16 TK. MAKE 2

LEG 1/4 TK. MAKE 1

1/16 DIA. HOLE

20

SPACER
1/16 TK. MAKE 2

FRAME
1/16 TK – MAKE 2

ENLARGE 150%

QUEEN ANN MIRROR

SCROLL PATTERN
3/16 X 10 1/2 – 7 1/2
MAKE 1

SCROLL

FRAME ASSEMBLY

ASSEMBLY

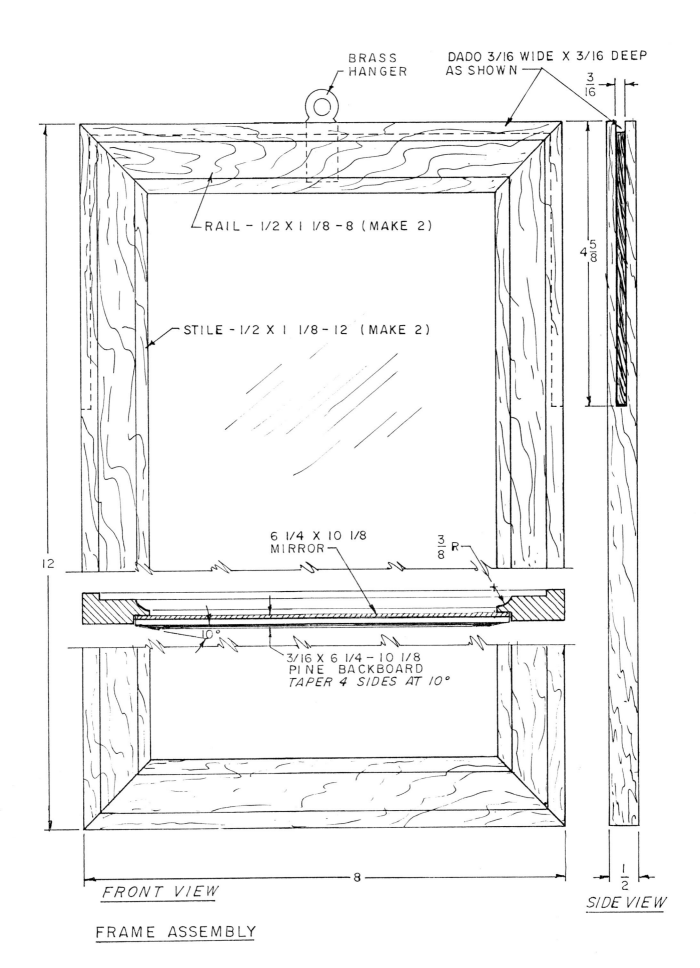

BRASS
HANGER

DADO 3/16 WIDE X 3/16 DEEP
AS SHOWN

3/16

RAIL - 1/2 X 1 1/8 - 8 (MAKE 2)

4 5/8

STILE - 1/2 X 1 1/8 - 12 (MAKE 2)

6 1/4 X 10 1/8
MIRROR

3/8 R

10°

3/16 X 6 1/4 - 10 1/8
PINE BACKBOARD
TAPER 4 SIDES AT 10°

12

8

FRONT VIEW

1/2

SIDE VIEW

FRAME ASSEMBLY

Appendix 'A'

Where To Get Clock Parts and Hardware

(These are the names/addresses we know of at this time any omissions
are only because we do not know of them or simply we "goofed".) Write
them for their catalog - tell them the NELSON'S of "NELSON DESIGNS"
told you to write them.

In Alphabet Order:

Amor Crafts
PO Box 445
East Northport, NY 11731

Cherry Tree
PO Box 369
Belmont, OH 43718

Constantine
2050 Eastchester Road
Bronx, NY 10461

Don Jer Products (Suede-Tex-only)
8 Ilene Court
Belle Mead, NJ 08502

Innovation Specialties
11869 Teale Street
Culver City, CA 90230

Klockit
PO Box 636
Lake Geneva, WI 53145

Leichtung Workshops
1 Woodworkers Way
Seabrook, NH 03874

Meisel Hardware Specialties
PO Box 70
Mound, MN 55364-0070

Merritt Antiques, Inc.
RD 2
Douglasville, PA 19518

Precision Movements
4251 Chestnut Street PO Box 689
Emmaus, PA 18049-0689

P.S. Wood
10 Dowing Street Suite #3
Library, PA 15129

S. LaRose, Inc.
234 Commerce Place
Greensborough, NC 27420

Shipley Co.
2075 S. University Blvd. Suite 119
Denver, CO 80210

Sloan's Woodshop
3453 Callis Road
Lebanon, TN 37090

Steebar Corp.
PO Box 980
Andover, NJ 07821-0980

Turncraft
PO Box 70
Mound, TN 55364-0070

Woodcraft
PO Box 4000 41 Atlantic Ave.
Woburn, MA 01888

Woodworkers Supply of New Mexico
5604 Alameda NE
Albuquerque, NM 87113

More Great Project Books from Fox Chapel Publishing